REMARKABLE LGBTQ LIVES™

Rachel MADDOW

PRIMETIME POLITICAL COMMENTATOR

Rachel MADDOW

PRIMETIME POLITICAL COMMENTATOR

AMY HOUTS

ROSEN
PUBLISHING®

New York

Published in 2015 by The Rosen Publishing Group, Inc.
29 East 21st Street, New York, NY 10010

Library of Congress Cataloging-in-Publication Data

Houts, Amy, 1957–
Rachel Maddow: primetime political commentator/
Amy Houts.—1st edition.
    p. cm.—(Remarkable LGBTQ lives)
Includes bibliographical references and index.
ISBN 978-1-4777-7891-3 (library bound)
1. Maddow, Rachel—Juvenile literature. 2. Television
personalities—United States—Biography—Juvenile
literature. 3. Radio personalities—United States—
Biography—Juvenile literature. 4. Political activists—
United States—Biography—Juvenile literature. I. Title.
PN1992.4.M2595H68 2014
070.92—dc23
[B]
                                    2014006860

Manufactured in China

CONTENTS

INTRO

Watching *The Rachel Maddow Show*, it's obvious that Rachel Maddow (whose last name rhymes with the word "shadow") loves her job. Often smiling and sincerely excited about the news—something that others often find boring—Maddow breaks down complex issues into easily understandable parts. The first openly gay primetime news anchor, she has the freedom to present the topics about which she cares passionately, including LGBT (an acronym that stands for "lesbian, gay, bisexual, and transgender") rights, issues surrounding AIDS and treatment, and women's rights. Other news shows do not always report on these controversial issues, but Maddow is a natural at presenting them. In fact, it seems as though Maddow was born to host her own news show, even though she didn't plan on a career in broadcasting.

Maddow grew up during the 1980s, a time when AIDS (acquired immune deficiency syndrome) was a new, unfamiliar disease that, for lack of research and treatment options, was considered to be a

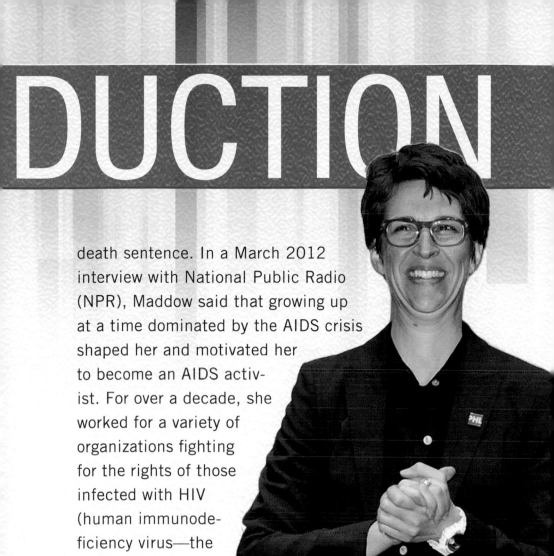

death sentence. In a March 2012 interview with National Public Radio (NPR), Maddow said that growing up at a time dominated by the AIDS crisis shaped her and motivated her to become an AIDS activist. For over a decade, she worked for a variety of organizations fighting for the rights of those infected with HIV (human immunodeficiency virus—the virus that causes AIDS). She fought for one of the most marginalized groups

An elated Rachel Maddow talks about her book, *Drift: The Unmooring of American Military Power*, at the 2013 Philadelphia Book Festival.

of people, those in prison who were infected with HIV. Because of the ignorance surrounding the virus, prisoners were unjustly segregated and isolated from other prisoners. At the time, Maddow thought AIDS activism would be her life's work. Among her most prized possessions are letters that she received from friends who died of AIDS.

In high school, Maddow felt a real connection to the AIDS movement, and she began volunteering. Looking back, she thinks her interest in the fight against AIDS arose because she was beginning to figure out that she was gay. Before fully realizing her attraction to women, Maddow dated a male marine in high school. Nonetheless, by the time she was a freshman in college, Maddow "came out," making her one of two openly gay students in Stanford University's freshman class of one thousand. She now lives with her long-term partner, Susan Mikula.

In spite of her support of same-sex marriage rights and the fact that the pair live in Massachusetts (which became the first U.S. state to make same-sex marriage legal, in 2004), Maddow and Mikula are not married. However, according to a July 2008 article in the *Nation*, Maddow said her relationship with Mikula was her "proudest accomplishment." She and Mikula have been together since 1999.

In a January 2009 interview with Lesley Stahl for the Women on the Web, Maddow was asked about being gay. She replied, "I don't often think about whether or not people know that I'm gay. I assume that everybody knows that I am. It's integral." Maddow's personal life and identity have proved to be major factors in her success and passion for topics that other reporters shy away from. What makes Rachel Maddow the person she is today, and how did her career make the transition from activist to anchor? The answers lie ahead.

CHAPTER 1

HERE WE COME!

Rachel Maddow was born on April 1, 1973, in Castro Valley, California, a conservative, middle-class community. The way of life in her hometown was quite different from the hippie counterculture for which nearby San Francisco

Beginning in the 1950s, people who embraced a new way of thinking that challenged traditional American values flocked to San Francisco and made way for protests, such as this one in 1984.

was famous. Rachel's mother, Elaine, modeled the advantages of a good education in her work as a school administrator. Her father, Robert, was a lawyer for a utility company. Her family encouraged her to help others.

A SERIOUS CHILD

Rachel's interest in the news started during her preschool years. A serious child, she began reading the morning newspaper at age four. Sitting on a kitchen stool still in her nightgown, she would read the paper while her mother prepared breakfast. By age seven, Rachel was asking her parents relevant questions after reading the newspaper cover to cover. That same year, she learned to ride a bicycle in one weekend without using training wheels. She was quite an advanced learner!

Rachel never used baby talk, the simplified speech many young children use while still learning how to speak. From a young age, she spoke using adult vocabulary. An articulate and vivacious speaker, communication is what would later make Rachel famous.

THE AIDS EPIDEMIC

In 1980, Ronald Reagan was elected president of the United States. Rachel remembers watching

Ronald Reagan's wife, Nancy, looks admiringly at her husband as he is sworn in as the president of the United States. Reagan was sixty-nine years old.

Reagan on their black-and-white TV set when he won the election. According to a November 2008 *Newsweek* article, Maddow recalled, "All I remember is the feeling of dislike." As she

studied the Reagan administration's policies further, her opposition grew. The Reagan era was marked by the beginning of the AIDS epidemic. This disease was first discovered by the Centers for Disease Control and Prevention (CDC) in 1981, and named "AIDS" in 1982.

Even though many Americans were dying of AIDS, President Reagan didn't mention the disease once during his first term in office. His budget also did not provide enough money for AIDS research, education, or treatment. With better funding, the number of HIV infections or the death rate from AIDS could have been significantly reduced. Because in its early days AIDS predominantly affected gay men—which at the time, and in many ways still, was a stigmatized community—many felt there was not as much interest in finding a cure for it.

An aide briefs President Reagan (*second from left*) backstage while his wife, Nancy, and actress Elizabeth Taylor *(far right)* look on. Taylor helped to establish the Foundation for AIDS Research (amFAR) and had invited Reagan to speak.

A former actor, Reagan had many friends in Hollywood. Nonetheless, he did not speak up about AIDS even when his good friend, actor Rock Hudson, died of AIDS in 1985. In fact,

President Reagan reduced the federal budget for AIDS research and care in 1986.

According to a 1987 article in the Los Angeles Times, more than twenty thousand Americans had died from AIDS or its complications at that point. In 1987, Rachel was attending Castro High School. That same year was President Reagan's third year of his second term in office. This was the year that he finally spoke about AIDS in public. According to an April 1987 New York Times report, President Reagan called AIDS "public health enemy No. 1" in a speech to the College of Physicians of Philadelphia. Soon after, actress Elizabeth Taylor convinced Reagan to speak at amfAR (the Foundation for AIDS Research).

However, waiting six years to begin addressing the AIDS crisis had major consequences. The delay in addressing the needs of AIDS patients meant that there were many more victims than if the government had focused on medical research earlier. By 1987,

GET INVOLVED IN HELPING PEOPLE WITH AIDS

Today, HIV is still a serious virus, but fortunately it is manageable with proper medical treatment. Following are five ways that you can get involved in helping people with HIV/AIDS:

An AIDS activist in the Philippines lights red candles in the shape of a ribbon, a bold statement of support, on World AIDS Day.

1. Support HIV/AIDS-related issues virtually by clicking on a social media link, such as following an organization on Facebook or Twitter, to help spread awareness. One of many organizations is (RED), at www.red.org, which was founded in 2006 by singer-songwriter Bono and activist Bobby Shriver to get businesses and people involved in the fight against HIV/AIDS.

2. Wear a red ribbon, which has been a symbol of awareness and support since 1991. According to the World AIDS Day website, the color "red was chosen as it is bold and visible—symbolizing passion, a heart, and love." Make your own by cutting a length of ribbon about 6 inches (15 centimeters) long, looping it around your finger to form an X that connects at the top, and pinning it on your clothing.

3. Donate your time. Like Rachel Maddow, you can volunteer to help on-site at an AIDS-awareness organization. Look online for local or regional organizations that can match you with volunteer opportunities in your area, or ask at your school or local hospital. You do not need special skills or a medical background to answer e-mails, distribute educational information, or help at an event.

4. Give a donation. First, decide which organization you would like to help. Your donation can be any amount, large or small. With the help of a teacher or parent, you can make a personal donation or get together with friends and classmates to make a combined donation. You can even take the necessary steps to organize a fund-raiser.

5. Choose a college major or take classes in public policy, medical research, an area of science, or another related field. These classes can educate you on how to affect public policy, raise awareness of diseases, and educate others. You may even be the scientist who helps discover a better treatment or cure some day!

most people were outraged by what was widely per-
ceived as the government's mismanagement of the
AIDS crisis.

A SUMMER VOLUNTEER

In high school, Rachel lettered in three sports:
swimming, volleyball, and basketball. According to
her January 2009 interview for the Women on the
Web, Maddow was a self-proclaimed "jock." The
5-foot, 11-inch (2-meter) teen had even hoped to
someday try out for the Olympics, but a serious
shoulder injury while playing volleyball ended her
sports career. Even as an adult, Maddow still can't
hold something in her right hand while raising her
right arm above her head. Though she was involved
in several high school activities, Rachel said she
always felt like an outsider.

While many social issues received national
attention in the 1980s, Rachel didn't feel a real connection to any of them the way that she did to the
fight against AIDS. She began volunteering at the
Center for AIDS Services in 1989, the summer before
her senior year of high school. Rachel would travel
about 15 miles (24 kilometers) north of Castro Valley
to the city of Oakland, where she would help with
child care and serve food at the center.

A person infected with HIV, which is the term for
the virus itself, does not necessarily develop AIDS,

the disease that leads to the progressive failure of the immune system. Rachel was more interested in helping patients with AIDS than those in the earlier stages of HIV infection because it was patients with AIDS who were terminally ill and facing death. She wanted those seriously ill with the condition to be treated with compassion and respect. That was the beginning of her life as an AIDS activist.

Although anyone can contract AIDS, the disease was initially associated with the gay community. A 2010 article on Examiner.com reflects on the early outbreak of AIDS, noting that the disease was initially labeled a "gay white man's disease." For years, there was no effective medical treatment for AIDS. Without proper medical treatment, those who are sick with AIDS often die much sooner than those who receive treatment.

A GRADUATE ON A MISSION

During her senior year in high school, Rachel attended the prom with her serious boyfriend at the time. He wore his marine uniform, and she wore a powder blue dress. For those who watch Maddow today, whose outfits tend not to conform with stereotypical expectations of what women should wear, the thought of teenaged Rachel in a powder blue dress seems funny. In fact, thinking of her prom photos, she now describes them as "hilarious" and her dress as "dorky." Maddow's later advice on high school, as expressed in her interview of actress Jane Lynch on the May 16, 2012, episode of *The Rachel Maddow Show*, was that "popularity in junior high and high school doesn't buy you anything in later life. And then I hear really you ought to look for the kids who are—like the dorkier you are at those important ages, the cooler you are probably going to be as an adult."

Soon after Rachel graduated from high school in 1990, nearly ten million people had become infected with HIV worldwide and more than one million were infected in the United States alone. At her graduation, Rachel was not the class valedictorian, but she was given special permission by the school board to give a speech. Rachel didn't specifically talk about the HIV/AIDS epidemic in her high school graduation speech, but she did ask for a call to action. In her graduation speech, which can be found on YouTube, Rachel rallied her fellow students:

> *We're living in the San Francisco Bay Area and this community is still pushing to ban text-books and is still upset that there is not prayer in schools. We can turn this community around and let the existing oligarchy [a small, dominant group of people who rule] here know that we won't stand for that close-mindedness. We can*

make Castro Valley an interesting and exciting place to live, believe it or not.

Rachel noted the impact that young people can have on the world. She begged her classmates "to do more. Don't assume that things won't change here where you live. Make them change. I wish the class of 1990 the best of luck at everything we choose to do, and I warn this community, here we come!" In college, Rachel would make good on her promise to do more.

MORE THAN AN EDUCATION

I n 1990, at age seventeen, Rachel Maddow started her college career at Stanford University, a private university located across the San Francisco Bay from Castro Valley in Stanford, California. Stanford ranks among the top ten American universities, according to *U.S. News & World Report.*

COMING OUT AT STANFORD

When she was a college freshman, Maddow definitively figured out that she was gay. According to a March 2012 *Newsweek* article, she thought it was "crazy" that only two of the thousand freshmen in her class had come out. She felt it was an ethical choice and decided to come out in a confrontational way. In January 1991, Maddow made a poster announcing the news and taped copies in each stall of the girls' dormitory bathroom. She said she just wanted to get it over with, make a joke about it, and move on.

The red tile roofs enhance the beautiful 8,000-acre (3,200-hectare) Stanford University campus, which was once a horse farm owned by Jane and Leland Stanford.

At the time, Maddow felt she had to be authentic to herself and to the college community. Stanford was not as progressive and liberal as she had hoped. She wanted her actions to make a statement. Looking back, she is quoted in the *Newsweek* article describing herself as "90 percent attitude." In retrospect, she felt it was an obnoxious thing to do and wondered why she thought any of the other freshman girls would care.

Soon after coming out, Maddow was featured in a school newspaper article. The *Stanford Daily* interviewed both Maddow and another female student, the two openly gay freshmen on campus that year. Maddow had requested that the newspaper not print the story until the following week so that she could go home that weekend and tell her parents first. However, the story was printed before the weekend. Someone—Maddow didn't know who—cut out the article and mailed it to her parents. That was how they found out that she was gay.

CHAIN REACTION

Reflecting on this chain of events, Maddow understood it was especially hard on her parents. Her parents were not only trying to accept what was shocking news for them, but also working through the way in which it was delivered: not directly from their daughter, but announced to the world in a newspaper. They wondered what kind of daughter they had raised who would reveal something so private to the media before telling her own parents and family.

Maddow still gets emotional when she thinks about how she hurt her parents, mainly because she is angry with herself. It wasn't that she didn't want her parents to know that she was gay. She wanted to be the one to tell them. She realized later that she should have agreed to the interview *after*—not before—informing her parents of her sexual orientation. That way, there would have been no possibility of the article being printed before her family knew.

Her mother admitted that reading the article was a shock because of her Roman Catholic upbringing, but said fear for her daughter's safety was also a big concern. In the November 2008 *Newsweek* article, Maddow's mother said, "'It was worrisome because of the idea she would encounter prejudice and bias in her life—and I am sure she has.'" Maddow explained that ironically, it was her parents' religious faith that gave them strength and helped them work through their acceptance of her news.

In 2013, Pope Francis was reported as saying, "If someone is gay and he searches for the Lord and has good will, who am I to judge?" The pope's comment made news headlines because it is in direct opposition to the Catholic Church's official position on gays. According to AmericanCatholic.org, one of the main Catholic online magazines in America, "The Catholic Church opposes gay marriage and the

The first pontiff from Latin America—and the first to openly demonstrate a more open position toward the gay community—Pope Francis waves to the crowd at his inauguration mass at St. Peter's Square at the Vatican.

social acceptance of homosexuality and same-sex relationships." It is important to note, however, that the individual members of the church do not always agree with the official church position. Maddow's

parents are an example of that. Changing opinions and increasing openness, indicated by Pope Francis's comments, show a growing acceptance of LGBT persons.

Although people today are more accepting of gay rights, prejudice against the LGBT community in 1990 was a much bigger concern. There was also a direct link between prejudice against the LGBT community and the HIV/AIDS epidemic, as AIDS was widely considered a disease that only affected gay populations. Now—over twenty years later—Maddow's parents have proved very supportive of her, but it took time for this transformation.

LGBT ISSUES IN THE NEWS—THEN AND NOW

Current LGBT issues in the news are different today than when Maddow was in college. The following are examples of issues affecting the LGBT community both then and now:

The Changing AIDS Prognosis

- **1990:** An article in the *New York Times,* titled "AIDS Doctor Tells of a Fatal Future," features a doctor who accidentally pricked her finger on a needle that another doctor had used to draw blood from an AIDS patient. The infected doctor said, "I can see what's coming—infection, disease, and eventually death."
- **2013:** The front-page headline of the Missouri-based *St. Joseph News-Press*, "No Longer a Death Sentence: Couple Learns to Live with HIV," tells of a heterosexual couple that contracted HIV in 2008 but five years later (with the help of modern medicine) were "the picture of health."

Defense of Marriage Act

- **1996:** President Bill Clinton signed the Defense of Marriage Act (DOMA), which prevented married same-sex couples from receiving federal benefits available to heterosexual married couples, even though the marriages were recognized by their home states.
- **2013:** The U.S. Supreme Court rules DOMA unconstitutional. An article on the *Huffington Post,* titled "Rachel Maddow on Supreme Court Gay Marriage Rulings: 'This Is Now Decided as a Nation. The Argument Is Won,'" quotes Maddow's reaction: "This is the most consequential way they could have chosen to rule in a pro-gay-rights way. This is a very big deal ruling."

Same-Sex Marriage

- **1993:** A May 1993 article in the *New York Times* reports that Hawaii's supreme court ruled that a ban on same-sex marriages may violate the state's constitution.
- **2004:** A May 17, 2004, *Boston Globe* article, "Celebrations Envelop Cambridge City Hall," describes the scene following Massachusetts' legalization of same-sex marriage: "Hundreds

gathered around City Hall by early evening, some gay people planning to get married, some straight people showing support."

- **2013:** A December 2013 *Washington Post* article, titled "More States Are Allowing Same-Sex Marriage, but in 2014 Challenges Continue," tallies up: "Same-sex marriage became legal in nine states this year, bringing the tally to 18 states and the District of Columbia."

TV Pop Culture

- **1994:** Wilson Cruz portrays a gay teenager on the TV show *My So-Called Life.*
- **1997:** Three years after playing a single, straight woman on the sitcom *Ellen* (1994–1998), Ellen DeGeneres came out on an episode watched by forty million viewers.
- **1998:** *Will & Grace* (1998–2006) debuted as a popular sitcom starring Eric McCormack as a gay lawyer who lived with Debra Messing, a straight interior designer and his best friend.
- **2013:** According to an online article by GLAAD (Gay & Lesbian Alliance Against Defamation), "Where We Are on TV": "Among the 796 regulars counted this year across 109 primetime scripted television programs on five broadcast networks...26 are LGBT... while 770 are non-LGBT."

Ellen DeGeneres began as a stand-up comic before becoming an actress and talk-show host on television. She also supports various humanitarian causes.

AN OUTSIDER

While attending Stanford, Maddow had the feeling of being an outcast. She didn't feel like she belonged there and even thought that the admissions department somehow made a mistake in sending her an acceptance letter. She also suspected other students felt the same way about her. However, the feeling wasn't about academic inadequacy. Maddow felt as though she didn't fit in at Stanford because of her political views.

Majoring in public policy, it was hard for Maddow to be herself. The public policy program at Stanford was conservative. As a self-described radical, it was hard for her to feel comfortable in that type of academic setting. While Maddow did encounter a warm community atmosphere at the Stanford residential houses where she lived (including the Paloma, Chi Theta Chi, and Columbae communal houses), this didn't change the fact that, just as in high school, she often felt like an outsider.

A QUIRKY PROTEST

In spite of the negative feelings she encountered while at Stanford, and perhaps even motivated by them, Maddow applied herself. She took advantage of the great resources at the university and immersed herself in getting the education she needed to work as an activist. The campus provided opportunities for her to push forward with this work. Maddow was involved in a number of organizations on campus: the Stanford AIDS Education Project; the Lesbian, Gay, and Bisexual Community Center; the Stanford Homelessness Action Coalition (SHAC); and the Coalition for Dignity and Justice at Webb Ranch (a labor activist coalition).

Maddow also organized protests while at Stanford. Her protest of William F. Buckley Jr.'s presence on campus demonstrated her ability to make a point using intelligence and humor. Buckley was a popular conservative commentator. The *New York Times*' 2008 obituary of Buckley states that his "greatest achievement was making conservatism— not just electoral Republicanism but conservatism as a system of ideas—respectable in liberal post– World War II America. Mr. Buckley declared war on this liberal order."

When Buckley was a featured speaker at her college, Maddow knew that the majority of people in the audience would wear typical conservative attire, most likely suits and ties. According to a June 2012 *Rolling Stone* article, Maddow and other protesters wore signs that read: "Thank you for wearing a suit and tie in support of gay rights." They humorously subverted the Buckley supporters and their conservative attire, turning their outfits into a support of gay rights.

Like Rachel Maddow, William F. Buckley Jr. hosted a television show on which he interviewed politicians and authors, among others. Buckley's show, *Firing Line*, was broadcast from 1966 to 1999.

LESBIAN AVENGERS

Along with the volunteer work about which Maddow felt passionate, there were practical considerations in her life, too, such as earning money. The summer after her freshman year of college, Maddow worked as a waitress on campus for minimum wage and no tips. She described her experience to the Stanford University Career Development Center as a "panty-hose nightmare." For Maddow, who is not a morning person, the other major disadvantage was her work schedule, which started at 6 AM.

After that first summer, Maddow found internships or jobs more related to her field of interest. She said her most interesting summer experience during college was an internship at a health policy think tank in Washington, D.C. A think tank is an organization that carries out research and advocacy for a social policy or political philosophy. Maddow began this internship in earnest but soon discovered that a separate nonprofit agency had already completed the research project that she had been assigned. This provided Maddow with free time to pursue other interests while in D.C.

Her time was not wasted. Maddow started a Washington, D.C., chapter of the Lesbian Avengers. Founded in 1992, the Lesbian Avengers were a direct-action group focused on lesbian visibility and survival. Direct action—the nonviolent kind—included marches, strikes, demonstrations, sit-ins, and kiss-ins. The group needed help to grow and promote their mission. Maddow put her time in Washington to good use by promoting a local chapter of the group.

WHY ARGUE?

Maddow said that one of the main things she learned in college was to make convincing arguments. By her sophomore year, she consciously knew that one of her main goals was to learn how to persuade. In a March 2013 article in the *Stanford Daily*, Maddow is quoted as saying that she found that by developing an argument and then asking smart people to "rip it apart," or search for the flaws in her logic, she could discover how to make better arguments. This ability to subject her arguments to criticism and use that criticism to improve them helps Maddow in her life and career every day, and she recommends that others learn to do it as well.

Maddow enrolled in classes she thought would help her as an AIDS activist. Coincidentally, these classes were the prerequisites for Stanford's public policy program. What does a major in public policy entail? According to the *Stanford School of Humanities and Sciences Bulletin*, "Political philosophy and ethics form the foundations of public policy." Public policy "provides students with background in

Maddow's communication skills are beneficial in her life and work. She is pictured here at a luncheon hosted by then U.S. secretary of state Hillary Clinton in honor of British prime minister David Cameron in 2012.

economics and quantitative methods, political science, law, philosophy, ethics, organizational behavior, and social psychology." This background would be key to Maddow's later success.

In 1992, Maddow studied abroad. She spent a semester in England at the London School of Economics. She loved London and said that politics was integral to what the students there were studying. Within a few years, she would return to study in England for her Ph.D., a graduate-level degree.

HOW TO TREAT PEOPLE

Another of Maddow's accomplishments at Stanford was the completion of an honors thesis in the Ethics in Society Program. When deciding on a topic, Maddow noticed that people did not always treat others respectfully. She wondered why people sometimes act respectfully toward others and other times do not. Her subjects were people who typically treated others with respect and generally had a strict moral code. Maddow wrote about how people—even those with a strict moral code about how others should be treated—sometimes chose instead to treat others poorly.

Maddow argued that the reason was because others were not actually seen as people. Psychotherapist Tom Moon defines this concept as "otherization." For example, people sometimes "otherize" those infected with HIV, no longer treating them as equals and viewing them as inferior instead. Completing such a massive, ongoing project as an honors thesis gave Maddow confidence in her abilities as well as information to help in her work as an AIDS activist.

She earned a bachelor's degree from Stanford in 1994, majoring in public policy with a concentration in health care issues. According to a December 1994 article from the Stanford News Service, Maddow's professors praised her: "Professor Susan Okin said that Rachel 'has a sense of purpose and strength of character that I am confident will carry her far. She has increased my faith in the next generation.'" The same news release mentioned that "John Cogan, senior fellow at the Hoover Institution and former Reagan administration official who teaches in the program, said Maddow was 'one of the dozen best students I have taught at Stanford. I have never met any student who has her level of commitment and dedication to public service, bar none.'"

RIPPING IT APART

In March 2013, Maddow visited Stanford for the first time since she had graduated. When addressing the issue of selecting a college major, she discouraged interdisciplinary studies (majors that incorporate multiple areas of knowledge), stating that students should focus on one subject and study it in depth.

THE McCOY FAMILY CENTER FOR

ETHICS IN
SOCIETY

STANFORD UNIVERSITY

Visiting Stanford in 2013, Rachel Maddow was able to share her thoughts and make conclusions related to her college career with the clear-headedness of one who has experienced the real world.

A majority of students at Stanford major in technology, specifically computer science. Silicon Valley, the geographic location of major computer companies, is located twenty minutes from Stanford. Maddow acknowledged that technology was valuable but was quick to add that it was no more valuable than history, writing, or other subjects. Even though only 9 percent of Stanford students major in humanities, Maddow encouraged more interest in such majors.

Maddow had been invited to speak at Stanford as part of the twenty-fifth anniversary celebration of the Ethics in Society Program. Her honors thesis on how people are treated as others is now given to Stanford students to read and critique. According to a quote Maddow gave to the *Stanford Daily*, students assessing her thesis today continue "ripping it apart."

FATEFUL FIRSTS

After graduating from Stanford in 1994, Rachel Maddow looked into joining the AIDS Coalition to Unleash Power (ACT UP). This activist group promotes education and fights for better treatment and effective drugs for HIV/AIDS patients. ACT UP was organized as a catalyst for the drastic changes that needed to take place in the late 1980s in order to save lives.

There were two groups near Stanford: ACT UP Golden Gate and ACT UP San Francisco. Maddow didn't feel that she had the scientific background needed for the Golden Gate group, whose focus was on treatment. Few women worked in that area of AIDS activism at the time. Maddow thought she could help more with ACT UP San Francisco, which oversaw the Prison Issues Group. Progress was being made with improving accommodations for prison inmates infected with HIV; for example, hospice care was being permitted for prisoners who were close to death.

ACT UP PROTESTS

ACT UP protests were designed to get attention by taking place in crowded locations to garner media coverage. These were not quiet, nonviolent protests such as the peaceful sit-ins that occurred during the civil rights movement, in which black patrons sat at restaurant counters designated for white people only. Instead, confrontational protests took place in various locations in New York City and Washington, D.C. ACT UP members disrupted mass at St. Patrick's

For its twenty-fifth anniversary, ACT UP partnered with Occupy Wall Street in a march from New York City's City Hall to Wall Street to support universal health care and an end to AIDS.

Cathedral, a famous Catholic church in New York City. They appeared unexpectedly on the evening news in the CBS studios. They chained themselves to the balcony of the New York Stock Exchange. They even scattered ashes of victims of AIDS on the lawn of the White House. Hundreds of protesters were arrested. ACT UP members sought results, and after repeated confrontations, they got them. While their methodologies were very disruptive, they did get noticed by the media and the government.

These protests paved the way for ACT UP members to talk to government officials who could make the changes they demanded. These changes included helping fund research on AIDS and treatment options, speeding up the drug approval process, and lowering the cost of drugs to make them more affordable. According to the Foundation for AIDS Research, an early drug, zidovudine (AZT) was "the first anti-HIV drug approved by the Food and Drug Administration (FDA). (At $10,000 for a one-year supply, AZT is the most expensive drug in history.)"

FIRST JOB

Along with her involvement in ACT UP, Maddow worked for a nonprofit agency. In 1994, she was awarded a John Gardner Public Service Fellowship,

One of the duties Maddow performed when working for the AIDS Legal Referral Panel was testifying at the State Capitol Building in Sacramento, California.

43

which paid her a stipend for a year. She knew she wanted to work on AIDS-related issues. Maddow interviewed with several agencies in San Francisco and chose the AIDS Legal Referral Panel (ALRP), where she was employed as a policy assistant.

Working in the public policy department with one other woman, Maddow gained valuable experience. She lobbied, testified at the state legislature, wrote reports and press releases, and gave speeches—all in an effort to influence AIDS policy. While she was working at the ALRP, Maddow applied for both the Rhodes and Marshall scholarships.

FIRST OPENLY GAY RHODES SCHOLAR

In December 1994, Maddow learned she had won both the Rhodes and Marshall scholarships. Scholarship rules indicated that she could only use one of the two, so she chose the Rhodes Scholarship. According to the Stanford News Service, only 32 Americans were awarded Rhodes Scholarships that year out of 1,253 applicants.

According to the Rhodes Scholarship website, the estate of Cecil Rhodes, a British philanthropist, established a scholarship bearing his name for "future leaders for the world who would be committed to service in the public good, and whose interactions in Oxford would promote international understanding." In 1904, the first American Rhodes Scholars studied at Oxford University, England. Ninety years later, Maddow's public service working for AIDS patients had earned her this prestigious award. She was the first openly gay recipient of a Rhodes Scholarship.

The Stanford New Service release announcing the scholarship described Maddow as a "radical lesbian AIDS activist." How did this radical activist celebrate? She shaved most of her hair and dyed the rest of it blue. Twice. The first try turned out more purple than blue. The news release explained Maddow's gesture, stating, "It was a symbolic gesture to prove she has not sold out to the establishment." Maddow's connection to her culture and real people has always made her an effective public advocate connected to those whom she claims to represent.

In 1995, Maddow left the United States to work on her Ph.D. in politics at Lincoln College, a college of Oxford University in England. Working with ACT UP and ALRP on prison-related issues influenced her choice of a topic for her dissertation. The dissertation, titled "HIV/AIDS and Health Care Reform in British and American Prisons," focused on prison advocacy.

RYAN WHITE: FIRST AMERICAN CHILD INFECTED WITH AIDS

In 1984, a thirteen-year-old boy named Ryan White became the first American child infected with AIDS. A hemophiliac, Ryan became infected through a blood transfusion. At first, his doctor said Ryan had only three to six months to live, but the doctor was proved wrong. Ryan stayed at home for over a year. As his health slowly improved, he told his mother he missed his friends and wanted to go back to school.

Out of fear and ignorance, some of the parents from his school in Kokomo, Indiana, protested, and Ryan was banned from attending classes. These parents did not know that you could not contract AIDS from casual contact. Some people said that Ryan must have done something bad and that God was punishing him by giving him AIDS. Paranoia and a lack of education fueled such theories in the early years of the AIDS epidemic. In 1984, Ryan spent part of seventh grade getting his class lessons over his home telephone, rather than in person.

After going to court to fight for and win back his right to attend classes at school, Ryan was taunted and insulted by other students. The tires on his mother's car were slashed, and the windows on their house were broken. In 1987, Ryan, his sister, and his mother moved 20 miles (32 km) away to Cicero, a farming town with a small population of 2,500. There, Ryan was more accepted at his new school in large part because the student body president, Jill Stuart, had invited medical experts to talk to her schoolmates about AIDS. The students educated their parents. Once the community knew about the disease, they were able to treat the Whites with compassion.

According to the Ryan White page on the U.S. Health Resources and Services Administration (HRSA) website, Ryan didn't want pity and often said he "wanted to be treated like a normal teenager." He hung out with friends, attended parties, and even had a summer job at a skateboard shop in Indianapolis. But Ryan couldn't be "normal." His illness and his fight to stay in school had made him famous. He appeared on television, visited former president Ronald Reagan, and attended the Academy Awards, which honor the film industry. Pop musician Michael Jackson, who was also from Indiana, gave Ryan a red Mustang convertible.

In the spring of 1990, Ryan was looking forward to the senior prom with his date. But he passed away on April 9, 1990, at age eighteen, with music legend Elton John by his side. His mother received phone calls offering condolences from well-known politicians, including Senator Edward Kennedy.

A few months after his death, Congress passed the Ryan White CARE (Comprehensive AIDS Resources Emergency) Act. According to the HRSA, "the Ryan White Program works with cities, states, and local community-based organization[s] to provide HIV-related services to more than half a million people each year." The program provides money for a variety of needs in all fifty states. Funding extends to prison inmates with HIV/AIDS so that medical care can continue once they are released.

FIRST EFFECTIVE AIDS DRUG

In 1996 (while Maddow was studying at Oxford), a powerful drug "cocktail" was approved that made a real difference in the lives of patients with AIDS. This drug helped keep people alive and treated the formerly fatal illness as a chronic disease. Because of the medical advances that had been made and because ACT UP had done so much for white, urban gay communities, the organization became less relevant than it had previously been. Its early mission to encourage better research into treatment options and raise awareness had been successful.

Nine years after ACT UP was founded, the demographics of AIDS victims had shifted. AIDS still took many lives, the majority being gay white males, but it had also expanded significantly to affect people of color and females. The work of ACT UP continued, but its focus broadened to attract new members

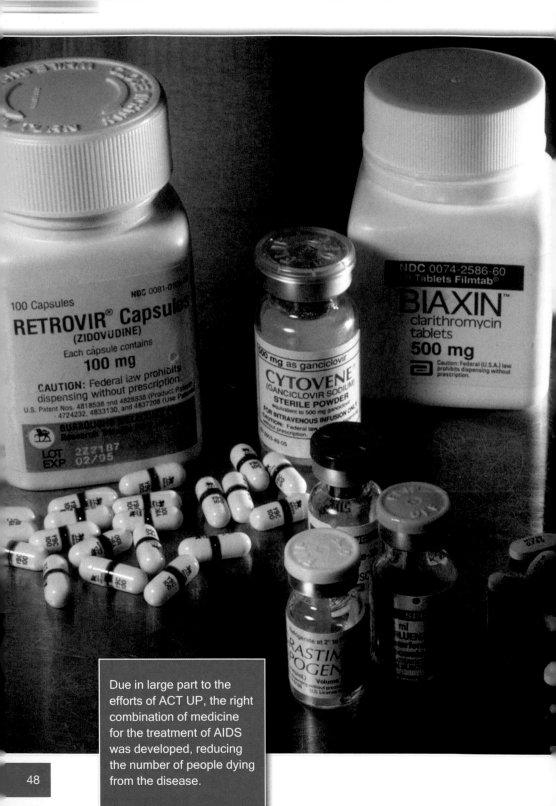

Due in large part to the efforts of ACT UP, the right combination of medicine for the treatment of AIDS was developed, reducing the number of people dying from the disease.

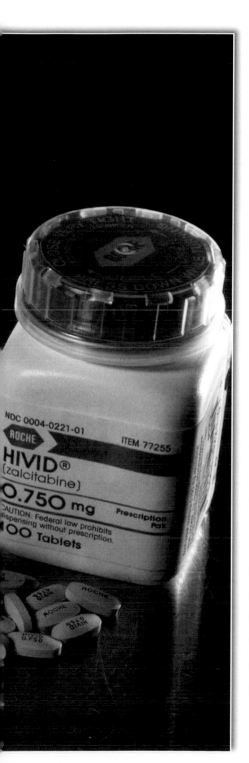

with diverse backgrounds and to include a global approach, entailing education, prevention, and health care access for all. On the April 27, 2012, episode of her TV show, Maddow congratulated ACT UP on its twenty-fifth anniversary. She stated that ACT UP had "changed the world" and that it "has a deserved place in American history."

FIRST DATE

In 1998, Maddow moved from England to Western Massachusetts to finish her dissertation. She was living with friends rent-free in exchange for helping out around their house. She could have lived at home in California, but she wanted to go somewhere where she would be able to concentrate. In a July 2008 article

Maddow and her partner, Susan Mikula, stand in front of Mikula's photographs at the 2011 opening reception at the George Lawson Gallery in San Francisco.

in the *Nation*, Maddow explained that she wanted to live somewhere she would be socially "unhappy" so that she could better focus on her work. She hated the cold, snow, and the countryside, so Western Massachusetts was the perfect place for her to concentrate. To earn money, Maddow took odd jobs, such as working in a coffee factory (where she cleaned buckets and stamped labels on bags), and more importantly, as it turned out, doing yard work.

In 1999, Maddow was hired to remove tree stumps for a woman named Susan Mikula. When Mikula opened the door, it was love at first sight for Maddow. The difference in their age—Mikula is fifteen years older—didn't matter.

Their first date was at the National Rifle Association's (NRA) Ladies' Day on the Range event. Maddow wanted to go on a date, and Mikula suggested they go to her sister's "club." At first Maddow misunderstood and thought it was a country club, but it turned out to be a rod and gun club—or a shooting range. Mikula was going to the event to support her sister. Maddow agreed to go as a favor to Mikula, whose sister is a lifetime NRA member. In a March 2012 interview with NPR, Maddow called it "the best possible first date in the entire world."

When Maddow talks about her date on NPR so many years later, both she and the host, Terry Gross, laugh. It sounds absurd for a liberal like Rachel Maddow, who believes in gun control, to be anywhere near an NRA event. However, Maddow doesn't believe that attending this event was in conflict with her gun politics. She is a good shot and believes you shoot at a gun club and leave the weapons there. While politically they differ widely, she has respect for one part of the NRA's mission: to promote marks-manship and conservation.

It was shortly after that first date when Mikula fell in love with Maddow. Mikula remembers the exact moment. They were walking in a cemetery in silence looking at nine-teenth-century gravestones. Maddow slipped and fell down on her bottom. Looking down at Maddow where she sat—that was the moment Mikula says she fell in love.

FIRST RADIO SHOW

Along with the other odd jobs she took on while writing her dissertation, Maddow decided to try radio. In 1999, a local radio station, WRNX in Holyoke, Massachusetts, was sponsoring a

This radio computer and mixer system is similar to the equipment used in the studio where Maddow was first a morning show host and later a talk-radio show host.

contest, holding open on-air auditions to read the morning news.

Maddow didn't sleep the night before her scheduled call-in to the radio station because she was worried she wouldn't be able to get up early in the morning. They asked her to come in to read newswires from the Associated Press (AP), an agency that gathers and distributes news. She was hired on the spot and started the next day reading the news on *The Dave in the Morning Show*. Maddow loved getting paid to talk on the radio, but she thought of it as just a job. At that time, after writing her dissertation, Maddow thought she would continue her work as an AIDS activist for the rest of her life.

AN INDEPENDENT ADVOCATE

Maddow also worked for the American Civil Liberties Union (ACLU) National Prison Project. Her work involved

political efforts to overturn HIV/AIDS policies in state prisons that discriminated against HIV-infected inmates. She traveled to the Deep South—the states including Alabama, Georgia, Louisiana, Mississippi,

Maddow's work in the prison system took her on trips throughout the American South and helped to improve the conditions for inmates with HIV/AIDS.

and South Carolina—where there were often the worst prison conditions. At that time, many states isolated prisoners with HIV/AIDS, but not those with more contagious diseases, such as hepatitis C. According to the online advocate for HIV-positive people POZ, Maddow found prison policies at that time "horrific." Working for the ACLU, she helped further its goal "to ensure that conditions of confinement are consistent with health, safety, and human dignity," as stated on the National Prisons Project page of its website.

Maddow took on many roles in her work as an independent AIDS advocate. She wrote articles, booklets, and fact sheets for various publications and nonprofit organizations. She also worked for the National Minority AIDS Council (NMAC), whose goal is to end AIDS/HIV by "developing leadership in communities of color" through education, training, and treatment.

Maddow's work and the efforts of other supporters throughout the 1990s and the turn of the millennium paid off. According to Dr. Elizabeth Kantor in an April 2006 report published by the University of California San Francisco, "Improved HIV identification and treatment in the late 1990s resulted in a precipitous drop in AIDS deaths among the incarcerated population [prisoners] as well as in the community at large. In 2003, a total of 268 state prisoners died of AIDS, down from 1,010 in 1995."

NO LOST CAUSES

Maddow was instrumental in organizing "No Lost Causes," a conference sponsored by the ACLU National Prison Project. Held in Washington, D.C., on June 17, 2000, the conference focused on state prisons in Alabama and Mississippi because both of these states kept prisoners infected with HIV/AIDS separated from other prisoners. The courts upheld keeping prisoners separated because they thought it would lessen transmission of the disease.

AIDS information coordinator Jackie Walker *(left)* provides information related to HIV/AIDS to inmates and listens to their concerns in the Mississippi State Penitentiary. Like Maddow, Walker worked for the ACLU National Prison Project.

The conference, a first of its kind, brought together 150 advocates—activists, lawyers, and scholars—to develop a strategy to help prisoners with HIV/AIDS and hepatitis C. It was important to help these inmates because the justice system was unsympathetic to their medical, physical, and psychological needs. Prisoners' lives were threatened in several ways, including a lack of medical treatment. Their segregation in work, classrooms, and housing prevented them from taking advantage of opportunities that were available to other inmates, such as reduced sentences and job training. However, it wasn't until years after the conference, through lawsuits and negotiation, that the last three U.S. states that still enforced segregation of HIV-positive inmates ended the practice: Mississippi in 2010, Alabama in 2012, and South Carolina in 2013.

While education and treatment have helped manage the HIV/AIDS crisis in the United States, the problem is global. The fight is nowhere near its end. According to the World Health Organization (WHO), seventy million people worldwide have been infected with HIV, and thirty-five million people have died from AIDS since the epidemic began.

CHAPTER 4

CAREER TRANSITION

Maddow continued with the radio station for one year, and she found it to be a fun, low-pressure job compared to her activist work. In 2001, she quit her radio job to complete her dissertation and return to Oxford to defend it. She earned a doctorate of philosophy (Ph.D.) in politics, but does not use the title "Dr. Maddow."

A DUAL PATH

Maddow returned to Massachusetts from England a few weeks before the terrorist attacks of September 11, 2001. After 9/11, Maddow strongly desired to get back into radio to inform listeners about what was going on and what they could do about it. She contacted a local radio station, WRSI (a different station from where she had previously worked), and asked to take a weekend shift. For two years she hosted its morning show, *Big Breakfast*. Maddow was still involved in various AIDS-in-prison projects at that time.

AIR AMERICA

In 2004, Maddow was offered a full-time job on a
new radio station, Air America. The job required her
to move to New York City. Maddow left Massachusetts
thinking she would just take a few months off. She
didn't know how things would go, or if Air America
would even last very long as a station, but she knew
that she needed to try it and see.

Chuck D started out as a
rapper in the musical group
Public Enemy. He has been
involved in political protests
such as this one during
the Republican National
Convention in 2004.

Maddow began hosting a liberal talk-radio show called *Unfiltered* for Air America. She was unlike her cohosts, hip-hop artist Chuck D and comedienne Lizz Winstead. *Unfiltered* was canceled in 2005, but Air America offered Maddow her own politically themed radio show titled *The Rachel Maddow Show*, which she continued to host even after becoming a regular on television. It was one of Air America's

highest-rated programs, and Maddow's fan base continued to grow.

POLITICAL TV WONK

During the 2006 midterm elections, Maddow was a frequent guest on TV shows, such as *Paula Zahn Now* on CNN. An expert on political issues, she expressed her opinions intelligently and firmly, even when they were controversial. During this time, Maddow also became a regular on the TV show *The Situation with Tucker Carlson*, which broadcast on the cable news channel MSNBC. She often disagreed or showed another side to an issue, making the discussions lively and engaging. Maddow was a guest analyst and commentator on issues such as gay rights, terrorism, and politics. She began working exclusively for MSNBC in January 2008 and occasionally filled in as host on *Countdown with Keith Olbermann.*

THE RACHEL MADDOW SHOW

Months before it became a reality, Olbermann began talking about Maddow hosting her own TV show. It was the next logical step after moving from local radio to national radio, and then from a

Television host and sports commentator Keith Olbermann was influential in advancing Maddow's career. Here he is speaking at the 20th Annual GLAAD Media Awards dinner.

63

guest commentator on TV shows to a fill-in host. With the same name as her Air America radio show, *The Rachel Maddow Show (TRMS)* debuted September 8, 2008, on MSNBC. At thirty-five years of age, Maddow became the first openly gay person, male or female, to host a primetime news show on television. According to *the New York Times*, in the first six weeks of *TRMS,* ratings averaged 1.7 million viewers, with nearly a half million aged twenty-five to fifty-four.

Even though *TRMS* debuted in the heat of the 2008 election, Maddow didn't endorse presidential candidates Barack Obama or John McCain. Maddow doesn't feel loyalty to any specific candidate or politician. In turn, she focuses more on policy. In 2009, the *Washington Post* named Maddow one of the top-ten television shows of the decade.

FAKE BALANCE

Reporting the news has changed in recent years in dramatic ways. While news used to be told in half-hour segments each evening, now cable companies host twenty-four-hour news stations. However, the key difference is the news slant. MSNBC, Maddow's station, is known as liberal, left-leaning, and supportive of Democrat candidates. In contrast, Fox News Channel is known as conservative, right-leaning, and supportive of Republicans and the Tea Party.

In simple terms, a political issue has two sides: pro (meaning "supportive") and con (meaning "against"). Of course, most stories are more complicated. But many people don't look at the larger picture, so they tend to be either for or against a controversial issue such as gun control or gay rights. However, some news stations present two sides of an issue that in reality doesn't even have two sides—for example, climate change (also called global warming). While the scientific community almost entirely affirms that climate change is a scientific fact, some news stations debate these proven facts as if they were untrue.

Maddow calls this type of reporting "fake balance." In an interview with NPR, she said, "It used to be that we agreed on the basic facts that we were fighting over, and we had different opinions about them. Now I think we accept different sources of authority." A major focus of Maddow's show is debunking this type of fake balance and questionable reporting.

SIXTEEN-HOUR DAYS

How does Maddow prepare for her show? She starts early at the MSNBC office at 30 Rockefeller Center in New York City. She works long days, often sixteen hours. Each day, she reads for about eight hours,

Rachel Maddow works in a famous seventy-story skyscraper known as the GE Building, which is located at 30 Rockefeller Center in the center of midtown Manhattan.

breaking to meet with her team at 2 PM to discuss which stories they will feature on the evening show. The work of her vibrant news team, who are mostly in their twenties and thirties, helps to target viewers between the ages of twenty-five to fifty-four, the age range she focuses on.

Because her show is different from most other news shows, Maddow had to train an energetic news team. They collect facts and ask important figures to interview on the show. Her guests are often experts on a topic or issue who provide knowledge and details on that topic. Because of the network's left slant, it is often hard to book conservative guests. They don't want to be associated with Rachel Maddow or her show. Maddow is concerned that for such guests, the mere fact of being on her show could become the story itself, rather than the news event or issue she and the guest are discussing. In fact, Maddow says that as her show has developed its following, booking a Republican senator is no longer even a possibility.

Maddow and her news team prepare for a long segment that lasts eighteen minutes at the beginning of each show. She begins with a topic the audience probably doesn't know about, gives background using TV footage and her own explanations, and then refers to the relevant event being covered at that time in the news. This differs from many other shows, where a news anchor typically starts with the current news and then adds the background details afterward. But

Maddow likes to lead her viewers and keep them eager to see where she is headed with a talking point. She helps her audience picture something new and tries to persuade them to see her point of view.

In addition to the interviews and hard news with in-depth coverage, Maddow and her team also prepare some less serious segments. Maddow lists both true and false statements and asks viewers to guess whether they are true or false in a section of the show called "Debunction Junction." Viewers hear heartwarming stories in another segment called "Best New Thing in the World."

Maddow and her team write and edit the script for the hour-long show on the day it will air. By 9 PM, *TRMS* begins, and sometimes they aren't quite ready. When that occurs, the audience will see Maddow sitting with a stack of papers, writing to catch up as the show cuts to a commercial break.

ON AIR

Maddow is not the typical, serious, even-tempered news anchor or a hard-nosed, angry news anchor. Many find her to be completely refreshing. She talks to her audience as if they are her friends. Because of this tone, Maddow's audience is no longer simply

Maddow prepares for *The Rachel Maddow Show* while sitting at her desk. The camera shoots a wide angle of the set, rather than using close headshots as other news shows do.

listening; they are engaged, waiting to see what she will reveal next about the story and the reason she chose this particular topic out of all the other news of the day. That's one reason why *TRMS* has won a number of prestigious awards.

While the show is airing, Maddow's producer, Bill Wolff, checks the social media website Twitter. There, he can quickly see how viewers are reacting. Wolff says viewers respond the most when Maddow is defending any type of rights: women's, voting, or health care. Maddow herself is incredibly passionate about discussing these rights.

One example is from December 2013. Signing up for the U.S. health insurance mandate was still in the early stages, and at this time, the federal government's Affordable Care Act website was giving people lots of trouble. While Maddow doesn't usually criticize other news stations, she could not let a falsehood reported on Fox News related to an issue about which she feels passionate go unchallenged. She studied health care policy at Stanford and has championed health care coverage her whole adult life, not only for HIV/AIDS patients, but for everyone.

Smiling, Maddow reported about a father who told Fox News that the Affordable Care Act (commonly called "Obamacare") doesn't provide health care coverage for babies. The interviewed father said that his eighteen-month-old baby was not covered by Obamacare, while his three older children indeed were. Because of their bias against Democratic president Barack Obama, Fox News omitted that the father forgot to write his baby's name on the application and that this was the reason his eighteen-month-old was not covered. Maddow showed her

FIGHT LGBT DISCRIMINATION

Every person, no matter what age, has the right to be treated with respect. But sometimes people are targeted because of the way they talk, the clothes they wear, or because they are LGBT.

You might have heard that in countries like the United States and Canada, there is equality under the law. Unfortunately, this is not completely true. Laws still allow some forms of discrimination. In many states, it is legal to fire someone who is LGBT or is presumed to be, even if he or she is a good worker. However, there are laws prohibiting harassment in public schools.

There are several forms of discrimination related to harassment, privacy, and freedom of speech. Do your classmates call you names or threaten you? Has a grownup, classmate, or even a friend told others that you are gay when you did not want him or her to? Does your school prevent you from talking about being gay or wearing a gay pride T-shirt? If you are discriminated against, there are a number of ways you can take action. You might try to handle it yourself by ignoring the person or asserting your opinion, but sometimes you need to tell a trusted adult.

1. If it happens on the bus or in school, tell your guidance counselor, assistant principal, or principal. If you attend a public school, your school is obligated to take action. According to the U.S. Department of Education Office for Civil Rights, "If harassment has occurred, a school must take prompt and effective steps reasonably calculated to end the harassment, eliminate any hostile environment, and prevent its recurrence." If you attend a private school, you should ask a trusted adult about the school's antibullying or antidiscrimination policies.

2. Keep a record of the incident by writing down what happened, where it happened, who was involved, and if a teacher or other adult was present. Keep your records in a safe place.

3. If you confided in your parents and they are supportive, tell them what is happening. If not, find another adult advocate, such as a relative or clergy person. Show him or her your records. Ask if he or she can go with you to meet your school's guidance counselor.

(continued on the next page)

(continued from the previous page)

4. Evaluate the outcome and how you are feeling. Are the incidents continuing? Do you experience anxiety at the location of the incident? Report each incident to your school counselor.
5. If discrimination is continuing, you and a trusted adult can write a letter to the principal.
6. If the process isn't working, you could contact the U.S. Department of Education or the American Civil Liberties Union (ACLU). The ACLU says, "Get in touch with us if your school isn't helping fix the problem. We've had a lot of success in getting schools to do something about the harassment even without going to court."

passion for health care rights by debunking the Fox News story.

FASHION STATEMENT

What some viewers may not realize about the way Maddow dresses for *TRMS* is that she wears jeans and sneakers. Of course, you can't see them because she sits behind a table. All her viewers see is a neutral-colored suit jacket and a scoop-neck shirt. She strives to look professional so that nothing distracts from what she is saying. A brunette, her short, stylish hair is neatly groomed. On *TRMS*, she wears contact lenses, but catch her on any other TV show, and she'll be wearing chunky glasses. *Rolling Stone* once described her as a "full-on nerd."

AN ACTIVIST?

An activist feels strongly either for or against a contro-versial issue. That gives him or her the power to act. According to POZ, Maddow defined activism as "figur-ing out there is something that you want to be changed in the world." Once a person figures out what it is that he or she wants to change, it is time to figure out how to make that change happen. Maddow says she isn't an activist anymore. She sees a big distinction between activism and broadcasting. Broadcasting is imparting information and raising awareness. She doesn't tell people to call their congressperson to pass a bill or fight for a cause. She only makes exceptions when an issue relates to AIDS, the cause for which she previously worked as a dedicated activist.

Maddow explains that she is trying to understand the world herself. Figuring out how to explain the news to her viewers helps with the process. In fact, she can usually boil down a complex topic into a short, ear-catching phase. Maddow makes the dis-tinction that informing is not the same as trying to change something or win something. Changing things is the goal of an activist.

REPORTING ON AIDS

Maddow loves the fact that as the host of *TRMS*, she can choose what topics she will cover. Story selection is integral to the control she has on the show. She reports about the AIDS movement even when other media outlets don't or won't because they feel it's too controversial. On the AIDS activist site POZ, Maddow is quoted as saying, "I think that the AIDS movement is part of what more Americans should think of as a successful way to be a civic-minded American." The AIDS movement brought about real change for members of the community and a concern for the public good.

While Maddow is not currently in the field work-ing directly with inmates with HIV/AIDS, she is broadcasting the necessary facts so that others can become activists. She not only reports but also gives urgency to an issue, which in turn helps people in need. One example is when she paid tribute to the passing of Martin Delaney, the leader of Project Inform, an organization that helped changed the way medical research was carried out for patients with HIV/AIDS, ultimately saving hundreds of thousands of lives. In a video clip titled "Tribute to Martin Delaney," Maddow ended her tribute with a call to action: "It is worth knowing about. Maybe even worth joining up."

NO ANIMOSITY

Maddow is different from other news anchors on television in that she argues courteously even when she disagrees with a guest whom she is interviewing. Some other news anchors shout, while Maddow exhibits self-control. Other news shows, even those on MSNBC, invite guests of different political parties or opposite opinions, knowing that they will argue with each other. These heated discussions draw viewers who are expected to agree either with one guest or the other. Maddow doesn't invite a panel of guests. She interviews one person at a time and presents her own viewpoint in a calm, thorough way.

Maddow respects other political views, and she is thankful to her guests for taking the time to be on her show. She wants guests to have a good experience on her show, so she doesn't interrupt or bully them. According to a March 2012 interview with NPR, she said, "I don't think personal animosity ever enters into it, even when I vehemently disagree with somebody."

KILL-THE-GAYS BILL

On December 8, 2010, Maddow interviewed David Bahati, a member of parliament in Uganda who introduced what was popularly called the "kill-the-gays bill," on The Rachel Maddow Show. According to Rolling Stone, when Maddow interviews guests, she "steers the viewer's attention away from the theater of politics and toward the exercise of power, which is to say, toward policy." That is one way that

Maddow successfully suppresses rage at a person who, for example, produced legislation that would sentence gays and lesbians like herself to death.

From the transcript of that episode of *TRMS*, Maddow's strength of character shines through in discussing this difficult subject. She directs her questions firmly and sometimes repeatedly, making her points clear and requesting information again if her questions are evaded. For example, at one point Maddow asks Bahati a series of related questions, "If you make homosexuality punishable by life in prison or in some cases by execution, what do you think will happen to gay people in Uganda? Will they flee the country? Will they become straight? What do you expect that they will do? What will happen to them?"

David Bahati's polite manner and calm, deep voice is disconcerting in light of the serious content of his bill to imprison and kill gays in Uganda, an issue he discussed with Maddow.

77

Bahati, however, doesn't answer her questions. He focuses on the word "execution" and requests that Maddow not use the word. He tries to distract from Maddow's questions and garner sympathy by describing himself as "a simple young man who lost both parents at the age of three years, [who] grew up as an orphan," and as "a God-fearing person." He emphasizes that his motivation to pass this bill into law was to be "consistent with God's law." He believes if this bill is passed, he will be protecting children. He says he has a "passion" for children.

Maddow addresses Bahati's comments. She asserts that she would never have implied he is on the same scale as infamous leaders such as Hitler. She then states that while Bahati doesn't want to use the word "execution," it is essentially a "synonym" for the death penalty. She also admits that she realizes Bahati said he would be willing to take the death penalty out of the bill. Yet, Maddow circles back to her original question of what would happen to gay people in Uganda even if the death penalty were taken out of the bill, but gay people were still sentenced to life in prison.

Bahati contrasts the rights of Americans with the rights of Ugandans. He doesn't just speak for himself, but uses the pronoun "we," to include all the people of Uganda. Specifically, he says, "I know that homosexuality is a human right here in America, but we don't believe that it's a human right in Uganda." He says Ugandans respect and understand the American perspective. In the interview, he also asks that Americans respect and understand the Ugandan side. He says, "If we take it as a crime, then anybody who is engaged in this...will face the rule of law." Bahati finishes his comments by stating the misconception that homosexuality is a learned behavior that can be unlearned.

In response, Maddow asks viewers, "Where do you think [Bahati] gets the idea that homosexuality can be cured, [that] it can be unlearned?" She encourages viewers to stay tuned to hear the answer after a commercial break. Following the break, Maddow explains her passion for the issue. Nonetheless, the interview was noteworthy for the calm tone and clear questions that Maddow presented.

For this type of reporting, Maddow won the 2010 GLAAD (Gay & Lesbian Alliance Against Defamation) Award for "fair, accurate, and inclusive representation of the lesbian, gay, bisexual and transgender community and the issues that affect their lives." For a former LGBT activist and current news broadcaster, this was a prestigious award to receive.

IN MY LIVING ROOM

The various TV shows where Maddow got her start, hosted by Zahn, Carlson, and Olbermann, are no longer on the air. Why does Maddow have longevity and high ratings that many other hosts, both male and female, do not? You could say it is Maddow's intelligence, balance, or credibility, but most would agree that it all comes down to one quality: Maddow is likable. Her viewers want to be with her for an hour every evening. It's similar to the reason why any TV show becomes successful. Does the audience want to spend time with the stars of the show and invite them into their living rooms day after day? Countless men and women, straight and gay, respect, admire, and like Maddow. She never thought she would become a part of mainstream culture or that it would even be an option. In a July 2012 *Rolling Stone* article, Maddow admits that she, indeed, has become a part of "the mainstream."

A COUNTRY LIFE

D uring the workweek, Maddow and her partner, Susan Mikula, live in New York City so that Maddow can anchor *The Rachel Maddow Show.* Their apartment is only 275 square feet (26 square meters), about the size of a large, 16-by-16-foot (5-by-5 meter) living room. Maddow once exaggerated, claiming that their black Labrador retriever, Poppy, takes up over half the space.

WEEKEND ESCAPE

After a tiring workweek, Maddow and Mikula escape from the city. Maddow is transformed from a busy, New York City TV personality to a relaxed, country homeowner. On Friday nights, Maddow, Mikula, and Poppy retreat to their Western Massachusetts home in the picture-postcard Berkshire Mountains. They drive 190 miles (305 km) north, which takes about three hours, and arrive at around 2 AM Saturday morning. In an

This photo of the Berkshire Mountains in autumn captures the unspoiled beauty, isolation, and remote location of Maddow's weekend home, the opposite of her New York City experience.

October 2008 *New York Times* article, Maddow expresses the advantage of a long drive: "It's an opportunity for me to turn my brain off."

Their country home was built in 1865, right when the Civil War was ending. They live near a state forest where Poppy can run. Compared to the cramped living quarters of their city apartment, Maddow enjoys the space and peacefulness of the country and their comfortable home. This is quite a change from her feelings in 1990, when she hated Massachusetts, deciding to live there to force herself to concentrate on her dissertation. Now it's a place where she can unwind, relax, and recharge for a busy workweek.

A TYPICAL SATURDAY

Without a need to look professional, Maddow wears comfortable jeans, colorful sneakers, and T-shirts under button-down shirts. Maddow doesn't sleep too late on Saturday morning. Among her morning errands, she takes Poppy for a ride. Being a large dog,

Maddow smiles as she holds up the book she authored, *Drift*, during a break at a book signing in Los Angeles soon after the book was published.

Poppy needs exercise and attention. Maddow brings him to a sheep farm where he likes the smells, sounds, and sights at the farm.

Of course, Maddow sometimes has to catch up on work over the weekends. She worked on her book, *Drift: The Unmooring of American Military Power*, for two years before it was published in 2012. She is also a regularly featured political columnist for the *Washington Post.* Sometimes Maddow uses the weekend to do preliminary work for her TV show. She reads newspapers, websites, and books related to politics and other serious issues. For fun, she likes to read comic books and graphic novels.

HOBBIES AND DOWNTIME

Maddow has been very lucky with a hobby she has practiced ever since she was a child: fishing. She fishes at the rivers near her Western Massachusetts house and carries her fishing license in her wallet so that she can go on a moment's notice.

In October 2009, a photo that Maddow had tweeted after she caught a fish on a boat near Cape Cod appeared on the *Huffington Post* blog. Holding up the fish to show its length, it was nearly as big as Maddow. The article repeated Maddow's tweet: "Have caught all fish in sea. Sorry! Ready to think politics again soon."

AN AWARD-WINNING BOOK AUTHOR

Maddow's views on the military were too complex to effectively present them during one of the brief segments of her hour-long TV show. Instead, she chose to express them in a book, *Drift: The Unmooring of American Military Power*, published in 2012. Maddow said her issues with the U.S. military had been bothering her for nearly ten years before she started writing.

Many members of Maddow's family have served in the military. Before Maddow was born, her father was a U.S. Air Force captain during the Vietnam War. Maddow might have considered enlisting in the military after college had it been legal for openly gay people to serve at that time. Her book makes the argument that for a number of reasons, there's a major gap between the U.S. military and American civilians.

Maddow argued that going to war doesn't affect the country the same way that it did in the past. The United States has one of the largest militaries

Maddow enjoys being goofy in front of the camera. She was visiting the University of Miami campus to discuss her book, *Drift*.

in the world and spends more on its military than the other top-five spending countries combined. Nonetheless, only 1 percent of Americans are active in the military. The families of those military members are directly affected, but the vast majority of Americans are intellectually and emotionally distant from the soldiers who protect them.

Maddow's book is not partisan. Members of both the Democratic and Republican parties have endorsed *Drift*. Roger Ailes, the president of the Fox News Channel, paid her book a compliment, stating that "*Drift* is a book worth reading."

Because Maddow is smart and well educated, it might seem that writing a book would be easy for her. Actually, she experienced high anxiety over the two-year period while she was working on the project. In a 2009 interview for the Women on the Web, she claimed her book was progressing too slowly. Maddow said she loves reading, but avoids putting pen to paper if she can. Given her dislike of writing, Maddow had to feel her opinions on the military were extremely important to write *Drift*.

Over the years Maddow and her partner, Mikula, have developed their own routines and hobbies together. In many ways, they represent a successful LGBT couple and are an example for others. Nonetheless, when asked if she wants to get married, Maddow has said, "I don't think we feel any urgency about it," according to an article in the *Hollywood Reporter*. Even though Maddow supports gay marriage rights, she isn't sure if marriage is right for her. She explains in the same interview with the *Hollywood Reporter*, "I worry that if everybody has access to the same institutions that we lose the creativity of subcultures having to make it on their own, and I like gay culture."

OVERCOMING A DIFFERENT ADVERSITY

Maddow suffers from cyclical depression, which she has lived with since the age of eleven or twelve. A chemical imbalance, she described her depression in an NPR interview as "disconnection...the rest of the world is the mother ship and you're out there on a little pod and your line gets cut...you sort of disappear."

Distractions don't help. Nor does her work. It doesn't take away from her energy or the joy she receives from her job. However, it does affect her ability to prepare for her show and the focus that she needs to meet the challenges and demands of the day. Maddow can sense when her depression is coming and knows to adjust her schedule for the next two days. One solution is asking a guest to host *TRMS* as she has done in the past and taking a break.

Maddow is also very critical of herself, so the way she performs on air can send her into a depression. Although she is open and honest about her shortcomings in media interviews, she doesn't like prominently displaying that side of herself. Even celebrities can feel insecure or think that they are failures.

SUCCESS TO COUNTER SELF-DOUBTS

While Maddow presents herself as confident and in control, she is often insecure about her television show. She compares and evaluates each of her shows and expects them all to be top rate, which is unrealistic for any show. After five years, she believes she should know how to produce perfect episodes, and any inconsistencies bother her. Her viewers might not notice, but she does.

Similar to the way she felt while at Stanford, Maddow admits that she wonders if people will view her as a fraud. But nothing could be further from the truth! Her ratings are the highest on MSNBC,

Comfortable enough with any audience to laugh and have fun, Maddow is seen here at the South by Southwest (SXSW) music, film, and interactive festival in Austin, Texas.

according to Mediaite.com. In a January 2014 article, Mediaite.com reported that "Rachel Maddow finished [the prior week] with an average of 325,000 viewers in [her target demographic], making her MSNBC show #1 in the 9 PM timeslot, ahead of Fox's Megyn Kelly, who had 305,000." The numbers don't lie, but they can't always change how a person feels. Summing up the description of her depression, Maddow tells NPR, "It's manageable, but it's real."

Maddow is an extraordinary individual whose personal and professional struggles pay off daily, not only for her, but also for the world at large. She has worked to improve the lives of those who are sick, and she keeps the American public informed and champions truth, debunking false authority as she goes. Rachel Maddow is someone to be listened to, respected, and admired.

TIMELINE

1973 Rachel Maddow is born in Castro Valley, California.

1980 At seven years old, Rachel begins to read the newspaper cover to cover.

1989 Rachel begins volunteer work at the Center for AIDS Services.

1990 Rachel graduates from Castro Valley High School.

Maddow begins her freshman year at Stanford University in California.

Ryan White dies of AIDS at age eighteen.

1991 Maddow comes out as one of two gay freshmen at Stanford.

1992 Maddow spends a semester studying in London, England.

1994 Maddow graduates from Stanford with a major in public policy.

Maddow is awarded both the Rhodes and Marshall scholarships.

1995 Maddow begins studying for her Ph.D. in politics at Oxford University in England as a Rhodes Scholar.

1998 Maddow moves to Massachusetts to work on her dissertation.

1999 Maddow begins a relationship with Susan Mikula.

Maddow wins a broadcasting contest to read the news on WRNX Radio.

2000 Vermont is the first state to legalize same-sex civil unions.

Maddow organizes the "No Lost Causes" conference in Washington, D.C.

2001 Maddow successfully defends her dissertation at Oxford to earn her Ph.D.

2004 Maddow begins broadcasting on Air America, a liberal radio station.

2005 The first radio episode of *The Rachel Maddow Show* airs on Air America.

2006 Maddow becomes a frequent guest on TV shows as a political pundit.

2008 The first TV episode of *The Rachel Maddow Show* airs on MSNBC on October 8.

Maddow is named the "Breakout Star of 2008" by the *Washington Post*.

The Rachel Maddow Show is named "Best of Television 2008" by the *Los Angeles Times*.

Maddow is named one of the "Top Ten Political Newcomers of 2008" by Politico.com.

The Rachel Maddow Show is named one of the top shows of the decade by the *Washington Post*.

2009 Maddow wins a Gracie Individual Achievement Award for Outstanding Host—News Program MSNBC from Alliance for Women in Media.

2010 Maddow wins a GLAAD (Gay & Lesbian Alliance Against Defamation) Award for reporting on LGBT-related issues.

Maddow produces and narrates a documentary, *The Assassination of Dr. Tiller*.

Maddow wins a Walter Cronkite Faith and Freedom Award from the Interfaith Alliance for her documentary *The Assassination of Dr. Tiller*.

2011 Maddow wins an Emmy Award for Outstanding News Discussion and Analysis.

2012 Maddow wins a John Steinbeck Award from the Center of Steinbeck Studies at San Jose University.

2012 Maddow wins a Gracie Individual Achievement Award for Outstanding Host—News/Nonfiction from Alliance for Women in Media.

Maddow's book, *Drift: The Unmooring of the American Military,* is published.

Drift is named one of 50 Notable Works of Nonfiction for 2012 by the *Washington Post.*

Drift is named one of *Kirkus Review's* Best Nonfiction Books of 2012.

2013 Maddow begins to write a monthly column for the *Washington Post.*

ACTIVIST Someone who takes action either for or against a controversial issue.

ADVOCATE Someone who works for a specific cause to promote change or raise awareness.

AIDS Acquired immune deficiency syndrome; a disease that causes severe damage to the immune system.

ARTICULATE To speak in a clear and effective way.

CONFRONTATIONAL Challenging in an aggressive or angry way.

CONSERVATIVE Believing in traditional values of society, politically referred to as "right wing."

EPIDEMIC An illness affecting a large group of people.

FATAL Of or related to something that causes death, such as AIDS in the 1980s.

HEMOPHILIAC One who has the disease hemophilia in which a person's blood won't clot, causing a prolonged loss of blood when injured.

HETEROSEXUAL An attraction between people of the opposite sex.

HIV The human immunodeficiency virus, which can lead to the disease known as AIDS.

HOMOSEXUAL An attraction between people of the same sex.

LEFTIST Of or related to the principles of the political left, which are liberal and progressive.

LGBT An acronym that stands for "lesbian, gay, bisexual, and transgender."

LIBERAL Believing the government should take action for social and political changes.

MARGINALIZE To put a group or person in a powerless position within a larger group or society, such as those with HIV/AIDS in the prison system.

OLIGARCHY A society that is controlled by a small number of people.

PARTISAN A member of a political party who adheres strongly to a cause or viewpoint.

PUNDIT An expert in a specific field who gives opinions in the media.

RADICAL A person who has extreme political or social views that are not shared by the majority of the population.

SEGREGATION The separation and isolation of a group, such as HIV/AIDS inmates.

STIGMATIZED Regarded with disgrace and disapproval.

WONK Someone with extensive knowledge of a specialized field.

AIDS.gov
U.S. Department of Health and Human Services
200 Independence Avenue SW, Room 443 H
Washington, DC 20201
Website: http://www.aids.gov
The mission of AIDS.gov is to expand the visibility
    of federal programs and resources for those
    with HIV/AIDS. The site includes relevant
    information, such as a timeline of AIDS.

American Civil Liberties Union (ACLU)
125 Broad Street, 18th Floor
New York, NY 10004
(212) 549-2500
Website: http://www.aclu.org
The ACLU fights to protect American rights and
    freedoms guaranteed in the U.S.
    Constitution. Its website documents key
    issues and actions taken in court and in
    communities to defend basic rights.

AVERT
4 Brighton Road
Horsham
West Sussex RH13 5BA
United Kingdom
+44 (0)1403 210202
Website: www.avert.org
AVERT is an international HIV and AIDS charity
    whose focus is education, treatment, and
    care. On its website, you can find an "AVERT

community fundraising pack" to help get you raise money in your community to donate to AVERT or another AIDS organization.

Canadian AIDS Society (CAS)
190 O'Connor Street, Suite 100
Ottawa, ON K2P 2R3
Canada
(800) 499-1986
Website: http://www.cdnaids.ca
CAS is a national coalition of community-based
    AIDS organizations across Canada. It pro-
    vides resources in both the English and
    French languages.

CATIE
555 Richmond Street West
Suite 505, Box 1104
Toronto, ON M5V 3B1
Canada
(800) 263-1638
Website: http://www.catie.ca
CATIE provides information about HIV and hepati-
    tis C. This organization connects people with
    health care providers so that patients can get
    the care they need.

Egale: Canadian Human Rights Trust (ECHRT)
185 Carlton Street
Toronto, ON M5A 2K7
Canada

(888) 204-7777
Website: http://egale.ca
ECHRT is a Canadian charity promoting LGBT
    human rights. The website lists activities to
    strengthen LGBT community, as well as a
    host of other information.

Foundation for AIDS Research (amfAR)
120 Wall Street, 13th Floor
New York, NY 10005-3908
(212) 806-1600
Website: http://www.amfar.org
The focus of amfAR is on research to end the
    global AIDS epidemic. Since 1985, amfAR
    has provided more than $366 million in
    funding and grants for more than two thou-
    sand research teams globally. Actress
    Elizabeth Taylor was its founding national
    chairperson.

GLSEN, Inc. (Gay, Lesbian & Straight Education
    Network)
GLSEN New York Capital Region
P.O. Box 5392
Albany, NY 12205
(212) 727-0135
Website: http://www.glsen.org
The mission of GLSEN is for students to be
    treated with respect, regardless of sexual
    orientation or gender identity. In local chap-
    ters across the United States, students,

teachers, and others can get involved to make schools a safer place.

Health Resources and Services Administration (HRSA) HIV/AIDS Programs
5600 Fishers Lane
Rockville, MD 20857
Website: http://hab.hrsa.gov
HRSA is an agency of the U.S. Department of Health and Human Services that distributes funds for the Ryan White HIV/AIDS Program. Federal funds are awarded to agencies located around the country, which in turn deliver care to eligible individuals.

Human Rights Campaign (HRC)
1640 Rhode Island Avenue NW
Washington, DC 20036
(800) 777-4723
Website: http://www.hrc.org
The website for HRC reports on the issues it supports related to lesbian, gay, bisexual, and transgender equality for Americans. Its mission is to change public opinion in America to promote greater equality.

World AIDS Day
New City Cloisters
196 Old Street
London EC1V 9FR

England
+44 (020) 7814-6767
Website: http://www.worldaidsday.org
This website features information about a global
    event, World AIDS Day, which has been held
    on December 1 each year since 1988.
    People unite in the fight against HIV and to
    remember those who have died.

World Health Organization (WHO)
Avenue Appia 20
1211 Geneva 27
Switzerland
Website: http://www.who.int/en
The website of the World Health Organization has
    a wealth of information related to health,
    health care, data, trends, and more. See its
    extensive alphabetical list of health topics
    and information.

WEBSITES

Because of the changing nature of Internet links,
Rosen Publishing has developed an online list of
websites related to the subject of this book. This
site is updated regularly. Please use this link to
access the list:

http://www.rosenlinks.com/GLBT/Madd

Boykin, Keith, ed. *For Colored Boys Who Have Considered Suicide When the Rainbow Is Still Not Enough: Coming of Age, Coming Out, and Coming Home.* Bronx, NY: Magnus Books, 2012.

Burd, Nick. *The Vast Fields of Ordinary.* New York, NY: Speak, 2011.

Dole, Mayra Lazara. *Down to the Bone.* Tallahassee, FL: Bella Books, 2012.

Farrey, Brian. *With or Without You.* New York, NY: Simon Pulse, 2011.

Green, John. *Will Grayson, Will Grayson.* New York, NY: Speak, 2011.

Griffin, Molly Beth. *Silhouette of a Sparrow.* Minneapolis, MN: Milkweed Editions, 2013.

Huegel, Kelly. *GLBTQ: The Survival Guide for Gay, Lesbian, Bisexual, Transgender, and Questioning Teens.* Minneapolis, MN: Free Spirit Publishing, 2011.

Hurwin, Davida Willis. *Freaks and Revelations.* New York, NY: Little, Brown Books for Young Readers, 2009.

Katcher, Brian. *Almost Perfect.* New York, NY: Delacorte Books for Young Readers, 2010.

Klise, James. *Love Drugged.* Woodbury, MN: Flux, 2010.

Magoon, Kekla. *37 Things I Love (In No Particular Order).* New York, NY: Henry Holt, 2012.

Merey, Ilike. *a + e 4ever.* Maple Shade, NJ: Lethe Press, 2011.

Moon, Sarah, and James Lecesne. *The Letter Q: Queer Writers' Notes to their Younger Selves.* New York, NY: Arthur A. Levine Books, 2012.

Moskowitz, Hannah. *Gone, Gone, Gone.* New York, NY: Simon Pulse, 2012.

Newman, Leslea. *October Mourning: A Song for Matthew Shepard.* Somerville, ME: Candlewick, 2012.

Peck, Dale. *Sprout.* New York, NY: Bloomsbury USA, 2009.

Saenz, Benjamin Alire. *Aristotle and Dante Discover the Secrets of the Universe.* New York, NY: Simon & Schuster Books for Young Readers, 2012.

Wilkinson, Lili. *Pink.* New York, NY: Harper-Teen, 2012.

Wright, Bill. *Putting Makeup on the Fat Boy.* New York, NY: Simon & Schuster Books for Young Readers, 2012.

Yee, Paul. *Money Boy.* Toronto, Canada: Groundwood Books, 2011.

Associated Press. "20,352 U.S. AIDS Deaths." *Los Angeles Times*, May 07, 1987 (http://articles.latimes.com/1987-05-07/news/mn-4605_1_aids-deaths).

Baird, Julia. "Rachel Maddow Comes Out on Top." *Newsweek*, November 21, 2008 (http://www.newsweek.com/rachel-maddow-comes-out-top-85007).

Boyd, Gerald M. "Reagan Urges Abstinence for Young to Avoid AIDS." *New York Times*, April 2, 1987 (http://www.nytimes.com/1987/04/02/us/reagan-urges-abstinence-for-young-to-avoid-aids.html).

Foundation for AIDS Research. "Thirty Years of HIV/AIDS: Snapshots of an Epidemic." amfAR. Retrieved January 20, 2014 (http://www.amfar.org/thirty-years-of-hiv/aids-snapshots-of-an-epidemic).

Gordon, Claire. "Act Up's 25th Anniversary Offers Chance to Reflect on AIDS Activism's Evolution." *Huffington Post*, April 27, 2012 (http://www.huffingtonpost.com/2012/04/26/act-up-25th-anniversary-aids-activism_n_1452597.html).

Heilbrun, Margaret. "Q & A: Rachel Maddow, Author of *Drift: The Unmooring of American Military Power*." *Library Journal*, March 20, 2012 (http://reviews.libraryjournal.com/2012/03/in-the-bookroom/authors/qa-rachel-maddow-author-of-drift-the-unmooring-of-american-military-power).

Hollywood Reporter. "Rachel Maddow Interview: Questions Obama's Re-election Chances, Gay Marriage and the Tea Party." *Hollywood Reporter,* October 5, 2011 (http://www .hollywoodreporter.com/news/rachel-maddow -questions-obama-gay-marriage-244494).

Ickes, Bob. "Maddow About You." POZ.com, June, 2009. (http://www.poz.com/articles/rachel _maddow_hiv_2331_16629.shtml).

Kantor, Elizabeth. "HIV Transmission and Prevention in Prisons." University of California, San Francisco, April 2006 (http://hivinsite.ucsf.edu/ insite?page=kb-07-04-13).

Karlan, Sarah. "16 Things You Should Know About Rachel Maddow." Buzzfeed, April 1, 2013 (http://www.buzzfeed.com/skarlan/16-things -you-should-know-about-rachel-maddow).

Lewine, Edward. "A Pundit in the Country." *New York Times,* October 17, 2009 (http://www .nytimes.com/2008/10/19/magazine/19wwln -domains-t.html?_r=0).

Michelle, Tona. "HIV/AIDS a Gay Man's Disease? Again?" *Examiner,* March 26, 2010 (http:// www.examiner.com/article/hiv-aids-a-gay-man-s -disease-again).

National Public Radio. "Rachel Maddow: The Fresh Air Interview." NPR.org, March 27, 2012 (http://www.npr.org/templates/transcript/ transcript.php?storyId=148611615).

National Public Radio Staff. "Timeline: Gay Marriage in Law, Pop Culture and the

Courts." NPR, June 26, 2013 (http://www
.npr.org/2013/03/21/174732431/timeline
-gay-marriage-in-law-pop-culture-and-the
-courts).

Plante, Hank. "Ronald Reagan & AIDS: A Legacy
of Silence." *Examiner*, February 6, 2011
(http://www.examiner.com/article/ronald
-reagan-aids-a-legacy-of-silence).

Sekhri, Aaron. "Rachel Maddow Visits Stanford for
the First Time Since Graduating." *Stanford
Daily*, March 16, 2013 (http://www
.stanforddaily.com/2013/03/16/maddow
-visits-stanford-for-first-time-since-graduating).

Stahl, Lesley. "Lesley Stahl Asks Rachel Maddow:
What Do You Do at 7 on Sundays?" Women
on the Web, January 29, 2009 (http://www
.wowowow.com/point-of-view/lesley
-stahl-asks-rachel-maddow-what-do-you
-do-at-7-on-sundays).

Stanford News Service. "Two Alumnae Win
Rhodes, Marshall Scholarships." Stanford
University. December 13, 1994 (http://news
.stanford.edu/pr/94/941213Arc4011.html).

Stanford University Career Development Center.
"Profiles of Success: Rachel Maddow."
Stanford University. Retrieved January 20,
2014 (http://cdcapps.stanford.edu/
stanfordcdc/fe/profiles_of_success/
posDetails.do?posRequestId=107).

Stelter, Brian. "Fresh Face on Cable, Sharp Rise
in Ratings." *New York Times*, October 20,

2008 (http://www.nytimes.com/2008/10/21/arts/television/21madd.html?_r=0).

Traister, Rebecca. "Rachel Maddow's Life and Career." *The Nation*, July 30, 2008 (http://www.thenation.com/article/rachel-maddows-life-and-career#).

U.S. Department of Education Office for Civil Rights. "Dear Colleague Letter Harassment and Bullying." U.S. Department of Education, October 26, 2010 (http://www2.ed.gov/about/offices/list/ocr/docs/dcl-factsheet-201010.pdf).

US News & World Report. "National University Rankings." Retrieved January 12, 2014 (http://colleges.usnews.rankingsandreviews.com/best-colleges/rankings/national-universities.)

Wallace-Wells, Ben. "Rachel Maddow's Quiet War." *Rolling Stone*, June 27, 2012 (http://www.rollingstone.com/politics/news/rachel-maddows-quiet-war-20120627)

YouTube.com. "Rachel Maddow High School Graduation Speech." Retrieved January 20, 2014 (http://www.youtube.com/watch?v=wd-IG2YoZUQ).

INDEX

A

AIDS
early days/history of
epidemic, 6–7,
11–18
how to help people with,
16–17
and prison populations,
8, 40, 45, 54–56,
57–58
AIDS Coalition to Unleash
Power (ACT UP),
40, 41–44, 45,
47–49
AIDS Legal Referral Panel
(ALRP), 44, 45
Ailes, Roger, 87
Air America, 60–62, 64
AmericanCatholic.org,
26–27
American Civil Liberties
Union (ACLU)
National Prison
Project, 54–56, 57

B

Bahati, David, 75–79
"Best New Thing in the
World," 68
Big Breakfast, 59
Bono, 17
Buckley, William F., 31

C

Castro Valley, California, 10,
18, 22
Catholic Church, 25,
26–27
Center for AIDS Services, 18
Centers for Disease Control
and Prevention
(CDC), 13
Chuck D, 61
Clinton, Bill, 28
Coalition for Dignity and
Justice at Webb
Ranch, 31
Cogan, John, 37
*Countdown with Keith
Olbermann*, 62, 80
Cruz, Wilson, 29
cyclical depression, 88

D

*Dave in the Morning Show,
The*, 54
"Debunction Junction," 68
Defense of Marriage Act
(DOMA), 28
DeGeneres, Ellen, 29
Delaney, Martin, 74
direct action, explanation
of, 33–34
*Drift: The Unmooring of
American Military
Power*, 85, 86–87

ABOUT THE AUTHOR

Amy Houts grew up in a liberal family atmosphere in New York and St. Louis. Several years ago, her eighty-year-old mother suggested she watch *The Rachel Maddow Show.* Houts soon became a huge fan and avid viewer, so she was thrilled to research and write Maddow's biography. With family and friends in the LGBTQ community, Houts is pleased to bring a positive message to teens. She taught writing for the Institute of Children's Literature. She is the author of over sixty books for children, including the biographies of geologist Meenakshi Wadhwa and composer Frédéric Chopin.

PHOTO CREDITS